Mel Bay Presents

Studies for Cajon

by Martin Röttger

1 2 3 4 5 6 7 8 9 0

Visit us on the Web at www.melbay.com — E-mail us at email@melbay.com

Preface

CAJON
The smallest drum in the world.
Don't want to lug your entire drum kit on stage? Want to play unplugged without drowning out your band mates? The cajon, the smallest drum in the world, is the perfect powerful accompaniment to any kind of band, be it blues, hip hop, boogie or rock: providing a full snare and rich bass sound, amplified or acoustic. Even complicated drum rhythms can be played easily – in your rehearsal room and on stage.

Little box, big sound.
This first cajon textbook for drummers provides beginners and advanced students with a step-by-step introduction to this little box of many tricks.
You'll not only find a collection of various rock and pop grooves, you'll also learn how to play drum grooves on the cajon in no time at all. At the end of this book you'll find a CD containing sound examples to the respective exercises to help you practice and control the sound you make. The CD also includes playalong tracks, allowing you to test your skills under realistic conditions.

Biography Martin Röttger/born 1970

At the age of 12, he was already performing on stage with musicians from the New Orleans jazz scene. Now Martin Röttger is one of the hottest cajon players in Europe. He was amongst the first to establish the Peruvian percussion instrument as a fully fledged alternative to the drum kit and thus accompany numerous national and international greats at over 600 concerts: from Louisiana Red, Chuck Berry, Toni Sheridan and Tom Shaka to Vince Weber, Chris Jones, Steve Baker, Rainer Baumann, Abi Wallenstein and Gottfried Böttger. Numerous radio and TV appearances at home and abroad plus several CD productions round off his success as a musician.

3

Contents

Introduction

About the Instrument

Playing Techniques

4

Notation

How the different strokes are notated

Useful Exercises

5

Groove Variations

Grooves with Breaks

Playalongs

Introduction

The Cajon

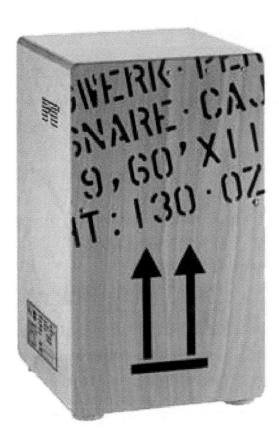

Many readers will already know what a cajon is. For those of you who are not familiar with the instrument, here's a brief historical outline:

The cajon (pronounced ca-hon) originates from Latin America and the name actually means "box" in Spanish. During the colonial era, slaves in Peru used wooden transport cases as a substitute for drums. Later this led to the development of the modern cajon with its warm sound and comparatively low volume. This is a rectagular box, usually made of wood, with a sound hole in the back (the side opposite the front panel).
It sounds similar to a drum kit and is played by striking the front plate with bare hands while sitting on top. There are four basic strokes, which are referred to as tone, slap, tap and bass. In addition, the foot can be used to dampen the front panel and raise the pitch of the tone. It's also possible to play using brushes. Some cajons are fitted with rattles, snare strings or a snare strainer.

Nowadays the cajon is an integral part of the modern percussionists' equipment. Internal modifications and improved construction have given the instrument an unmistakeable bass and snare sound which is now astonishingly similar to that of a drum kit. In recent years this has led many drummers to take advantage of the amazing opportunities offered by the cajon. It can be integrated into virtually every kind of music and allows the player to develop an individual approach by bringing in stylistic elements from drummers or percussionists as desired.

History of the Cajon

The cajon originated in Latin America and Cuba in the 19th century, during the colonial era. The emergence of the instrument is a direct consequence of slavery in these countries. As part of the destruction of the cultural identity of the African slaves by the Europeans, they were frequently forbidden to use their drums. One of the main reasons for this was that the Europeans were heavily outnumbered and were afraid drums could be used to communicate. The idea that information in the form of numerical codes could be passed over long distances was seen by the whites as a threat and they feared the slaves could use this method to foment uprisings or even revolution.
For this reason, the slaves began making music with tools or (in this case) transport cases. As these articles were indispensable for their work, they had the advantage that they couldn't realistically be confiscated.
The first cajons started life as transport cases for goods of all kinds. The different types of cajon emerged as a result of the different sizes and materials of the various boxes available at the time.

The Modern Cajon

Due to its convenient size and ease of transport, the cajon has increasingly come to be used as a substitute for the classic drum kit, instead of purely as a percussion instrument. For this reason, there has been a series of developments in recent years aimed at taking the instrument beyond its traditional role as a Flamenco drum and making it a viable replacement for a drum set.
Manufacturers now frequently incorporate a snare strainer instead of guitar strings behind the front panel, enabling a whole new range of sounds which have convinced many a drummer to switch to cajon for small club gigs or situations requiring only a minimalist set-up.
One of the leading cajon manufacturers is the Schlagwerk company, to be found in the internet under **www.schlagwerk.com**

Types of Cajon

Peruvian Cajons

1 Cajon Comparsa

2 "Two in one" medium

3 La Cajon Peru, playing surface
burl wood veneer

4 Hip Box junior cajon

5 Cajon La Peru, Sahara Wind

6 Cajon La Peru, playing surface
zebrano veneer

7 "Two in one" large

8 Bass cajon

9 Cajon La Peru, Black Eyes

10 Cajon La Peru, playing surface
beechwood

Models 2, 4 & 7 feature an integrated snare strainer.

Models 3, 5, 6, 9 & 10 are fitted with snare strings.

Model 8 is available with or without an optional snare strainer.

About the Instrument

What's inside the cajon?

There are a number of different ways to influence or change the sound of the cajon. These enable you to adjust the sound to suit your own taste.
Here are a few tips:

Damping the interior

The sound of the cajon can be changed radically by damping the inside with a cloth, blanket or cushion. An empty cajon resonates for a longer time, whereas by damping it, the bass becomes shorter and more punchy. However, if you use too much insulating material, the treble frequencies are lost. Personally I use bubble wrap, which is easy to apply and allows you to optimize the degree of damping to suit your preferences. New cajons are frequently packed in bubble wrap.

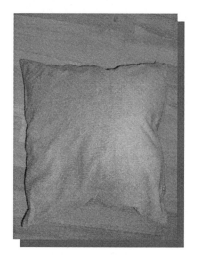 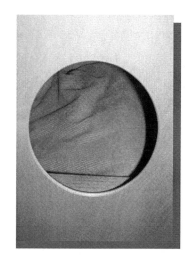 

Adjusting the front panel screws

This allows you to alter the volume and the degree to which the front panel rattles against the body. Through loosening the screws, this element becomes louder. By tightening them you make it quieter. In the case of cajons fitted with snare strings, if you loosen the screws then you hear the sound of the wood more strongly, whereas if you tighten them then the sound of the strings themselves becomes more dominant. Please note that this only applies to the screws in the upper part of the front panel - if you loosen the middle screws then the bass will lose definition.

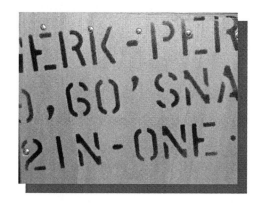 

Changing the tension
of the strings

The majority of cajons are fitted with guitar strings behind the front panel. These can be adjusted by means of two allen screws in the base panel. The looser the strings, the more intensive the snare sound. By tightening the strings you make the snare sound shorter and more aggressive, but try to avoid tightening them too much or they may break.

Modifying the strings
in the cajon

Undesirable overtones can sometimes occur in all cajons fitted with strings on the inside. This can be prevented by taping the strings with Sellotape or Scotch tap. Gaffa tape changes the sound of the instrument too much.

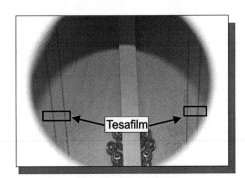

Cajons with snare strainer

Other cajon models are fitted with a snare strainer instead of the guitar strings described above. A snare strainer basically consists of a group of springs mounted parallel to one another and is traditionally found on the underside of every snare drum. This can be damped in the same way as strings. Cajons fitted with a snare strainer sound astonishingly like a drum kit. The "2 in one" model from Schlagwerk is a cajon where the snare strainer can be removed if desired. This variation enables both the traditional cajon sound and the drum set sound. .

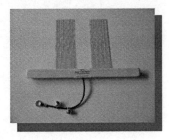

Playing position

Another unusual thing about the cajon is that it is played while sitting on the instrument. The player sits on the cajon as on a stool with the front panel exactly between the legs.

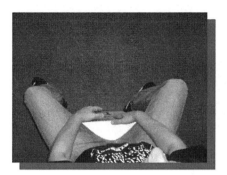 

What size cajon?

Cajons come in various different sizes. When sitting on the instrument, your thighs should be parallel to the ground.

  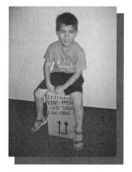

Correct size cajon   *Cajon is too small*   *Cajon is too large*

Tilting the cajon

The cajon is a lot easier to play if you tip it backwards slightly. It's important that when your back is straight, the degree of tilt allows your hands to reach all the way to the bottom of the playing zone. Like this you can produce the different tonal colours from the various parts of the playing zone simply by straightening your elbow rather than by bending forwards. In this position the body is in equilibrium and there is no need to balance it through pressure from the legs.

 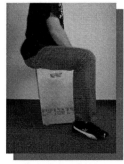 

Correct sitting position   *Too far back!*   *Too far forward!*

Where to strike the cajon

The usual playing zone is the upper one third of the front panel. There are two reason for this: firstly, playing the lower areas of the front panel can strain your back and muscles in the long term. Secondly, all the good sounds can be produced in the upper one third.

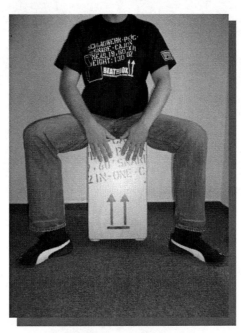

Correct playing position

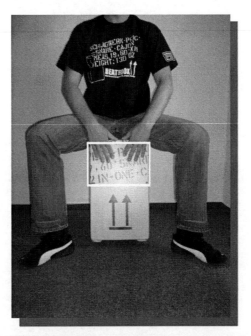

Only the outlined area of the cajon is played

Playing techniques

The basic strokes / sounds

There are many different possible ways of striking the cajon to create different sounds. However, we generally differentiate between four main types of stroke:
Tone, Bass, Tap and Slap.

The tone

The tone is the most frequently used basic stroke, produced by striking the upper end of the playing surface. On cajons fitted with strings or a snare strainer, this stroke has a short, buzzing sound rather like that of a snare drum. If the cajon is not fitted with strings or a snare strainer, the sound is more like a rather woody rimshot. You strike the instrument fairly close to the outer edges, so that the little fingers still just land on the front panel. The hands should be extended straight but relaxed and the impact of the stroke lands on the first joint of the fingers. The motion comes both from the wrist and from the elbow and all fingers strike the cajon evenly. The fingers can then rest on the playing surface if desired, as the cajon does not go on sounding like most drums

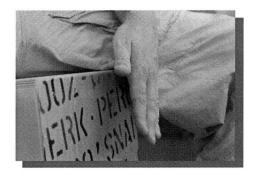

The bass

The bass is the lowest-pitched stroke on the cajon and sounds like a bass drum. When correctly executed, you don't hear any buzzing sound from the strings or snare strainer. The bass is deep and powerful.

When raising the arm to strike, the hand is stretched out in the middle and the fingers slightly raised but not tensed. This motion comes from the shoulder. The stroke itself also comes from the shoulder, elbow and wrist are stiff. The entire area of the palm strikes the upper third of the front panel in the middle and the wrist should be level with the upper edge of the cajon.

The tap

The tap is the quietest stroke on the cajon and is frequently used as a "filler" or "ghost note". The sequence of movement is very similar to that used for the tone, but the strike mode is more relaxed and lighter. In addition, the hand approaches the cajon more from the front so that the pressure falls on the fingertips.
The tap can be played at various different volumes. If you play it really quietly, virtually no snare effect can be heard. When played louder there is a slight snare effect, but this is not as loud as with the tone or the slap.

The slap

The slap is the loudest stroke on the cajon. In comparison to the tone it is louder and sounds more aggressive. The sequence of movement is the same as with the tone, but the hand is turned slightly and the fingers lightly bent. In this way the hand strikes the upper edge of the cajon. The impact of the stroke falls on the fingertips of ring and middle finger.

At first you should practise each type of stroke separately. Follow a bass stroke from the left hand with a bass stroke from the right hand. When you have mastered all four types of stroke - tone, bass, tap and slap - like this, you can begin practising alternating strokes. Here tempo is not as important as the correct sequence of movement and the sound. Practising in front of a large mirror is a great help in learning to control this.

Notation

A couple of explanations

In this book we use a notation system consisting of two lines:

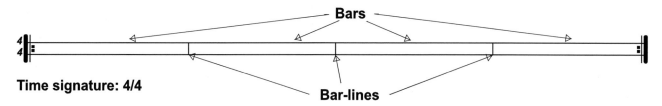

Time signature: 4/4

Every piece of music is divided into equal-sized sections called "bars". A bar is the basic unit of the piece. The bar-lines denote the individual bars.

Double bar-lines ‖ denote the end of a part of the piece or of a particular sequence of notes.

A double bar-line where the second line is thicker ▐ indicates the end of the piece.

The symbol ⁒ means: repeat the previous bar. Sometimes the number of times that the same bar is to be repeated is simply written above the symbol.

If an entire section is to be repeated, two dots are written before the double bar-line. This is called a repeat sign.

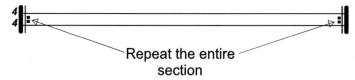

Repeat the entire section

We will be working a great deal with 16th notes. They are one quarter of the length of a quarter beat (crotchet) and are counted 1 e + e (spoken "one ee and ee". To help you count them correctly I've written this above every exercise. Which hand to use is written below the lines.

R = right hand   L= left hand

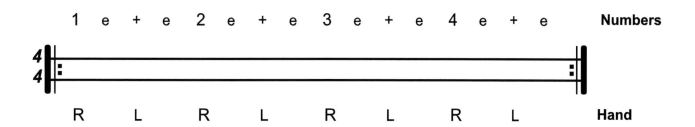

Several of the following exercises can be heard on the CD. These are denoted by the track number to the right of each exercise, e.g. 🄔

Length of notes (beats) and rests

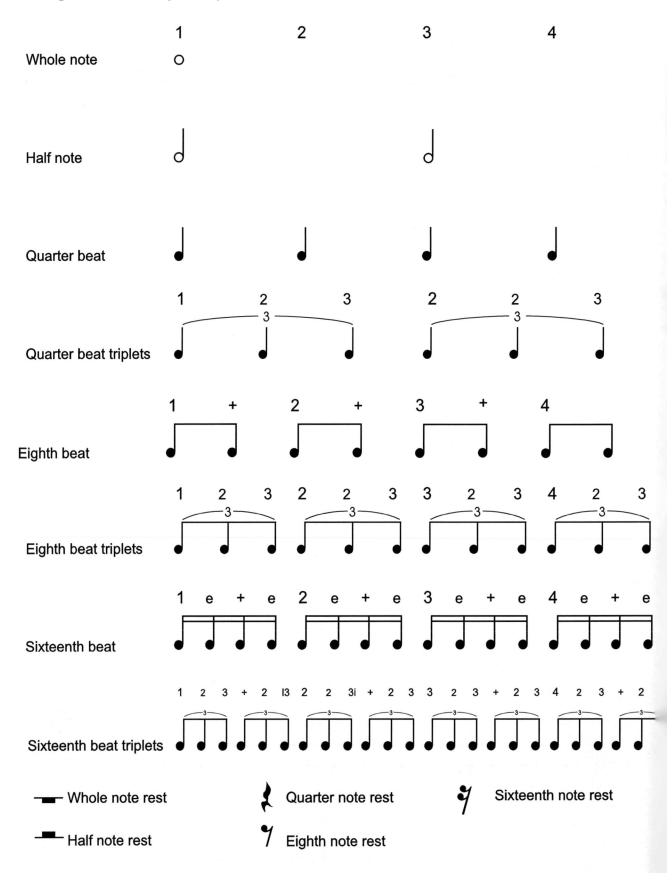

Whole note rest   **Quarter note rest**   **Sixteenth note rest**

Half note rest   **Eighth note rest**

The different time signatures
or meters

The time signature or meter tells you how many notes (or beats) of which length make up a bar. The upper number indicates the number of beats per bar and the lower number tells you their value or length.

4 Number of beats per bar
4 Length of beat

The note value tells you how long you have to hold the stroke for (or the interval until the next one).

2/4 time

In 2/4 time, the note value is a quarter beat and there are **two** of them in each bar:

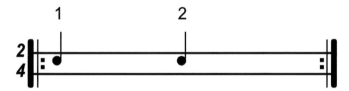

3/4 time

In 3/4 time, the note value is also a quarter beat, but there are **three** quarter beats in each bar:

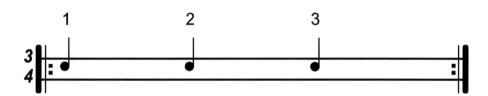

4/4 time

IIn 4/4 time the note value is a quarter beat and there are **four** of these in each bar.

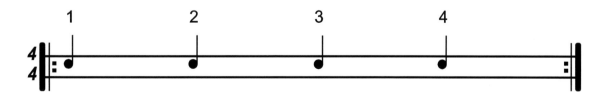

NB: a bar is a unit and is defined by the given meter or time signature. The most common meters are 4/4, 3/4 or 2/4. In each new bar, the first beat or "one" is usually played louder than the following beats. We differentiate between two basic kinds of meters - binary (2/4 and 4/4, both of which are divisible by 2) and ternary (3/4 and 6/8, both divisible by 3).

Extending note lengths

Dotted notes

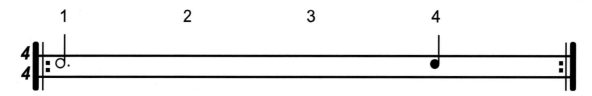

Note lasts 3 beats

The dot after a note makes it last half as long again

This means

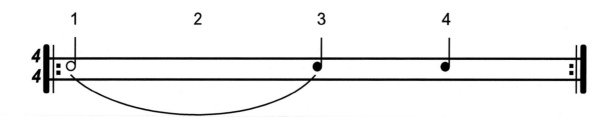

Another way of extending the length of a note is the curved line or tie. It joins two notes to make one longer note. This means that you play the first beat and the second doesn't sound.

Tie

How the different strokes are notated

The Tone

This is notated under the first line with the appropriate note length.

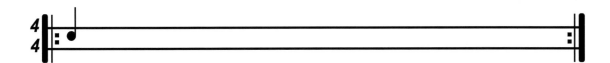

Table showing the different note symbols and lengths

Single note	Joined notes	Note length
○		Whole note
𝅗𝅥		Half note
♩		Quarter note
♪	♫	Eighth note
	3 (triplet)	Eighth beat triplets
♬	♬	Sixteenth note

The Bass

This is notated under the second line with the appropriate note length.

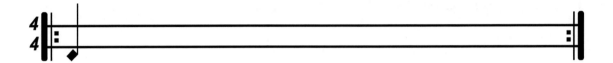

Table showing the different note symbols and lengths

Single note	Joined notes	Note length
◇		Whole note
		Half note
		Quarter note
		Eighth note
	3	Eighth beat triplets
		Sixteenth note

The Tap

This is notated under the first line with the appropriate note length.

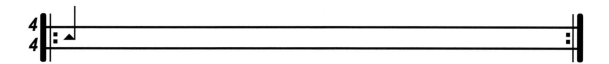

Table showing the different note symbols and lengths

Single note	Joined notes	Note length
		Whole note
		Half note
		Quarter note
		Eighth note
		Eighth beat triplets
		Sixteenth note

The Slap ♩

This is notated under the first line with the appropriate note length.

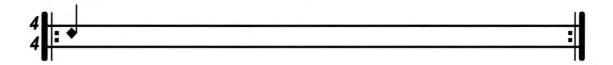

Table showing the different note symbols and lengths

Single note	Joined notes	Note length
◇		Whole note
♩		Half note
♩		Quarter note
♪	♫	Eighth note
	3 triplet	Eighth beat triplets
♬	♬♬	Sixteenth note

First Exercises

Basic exercises, getting a good sound

It's always important to concentrate on getting a good sound!
When playing the following exercises, try to find out how you can get them to sound best.
Check all movement sequences in front of the mirror.

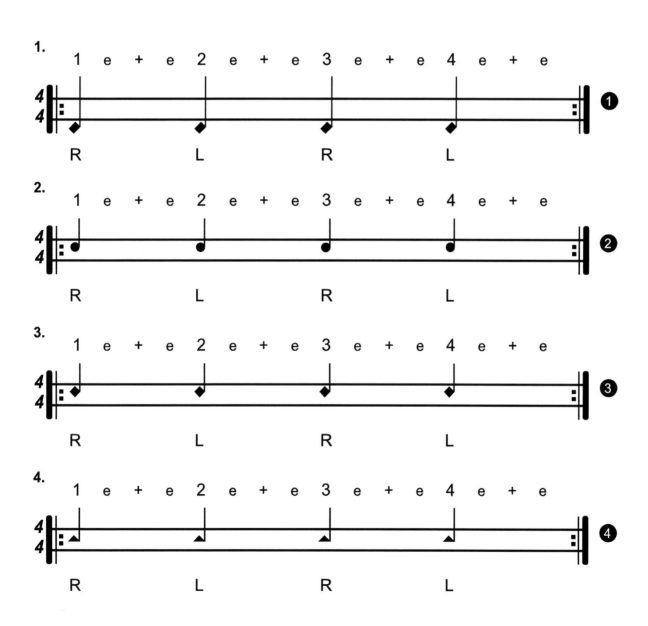

The staggered bass

The following bars each contain 3 tap beats and one bass beat. The bass beat falls in a different place in each bar. Count each exercise in and concentrate on playing the bass beat in exactly the right place.

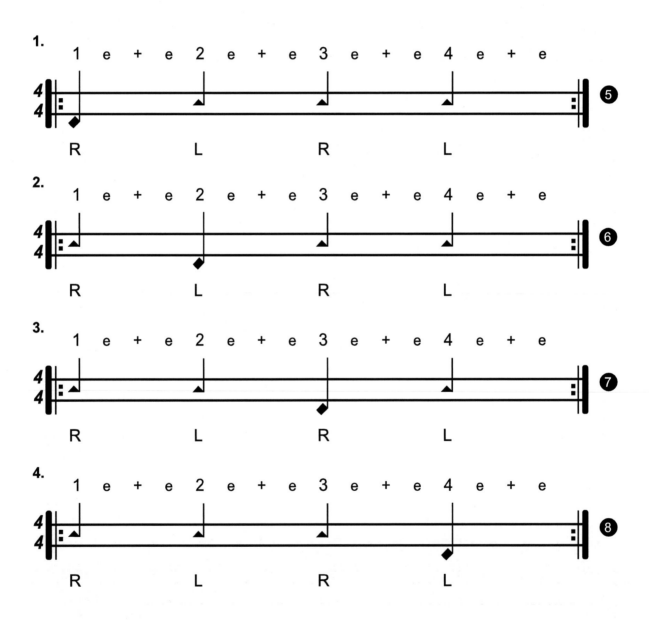

The staggered tone

The following bars each show three tap beats and one tone beat. It's a good idea to do this exercise with a metronome in order to retain your rhythmic orientation. If you don't do this, the mind can tend to automatically start defining the tone as the first beat of the bar.

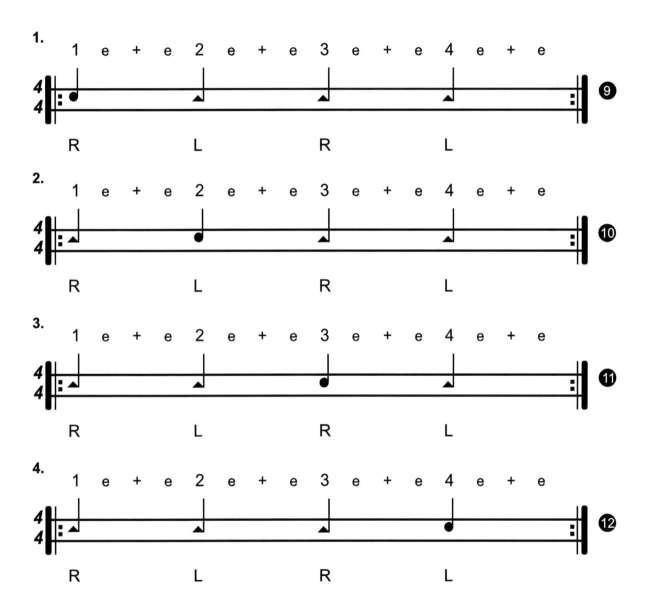

The staggered slap

The slap is the third cajon sound. As in the exercises on the previous page, use a metronome or count carefully.

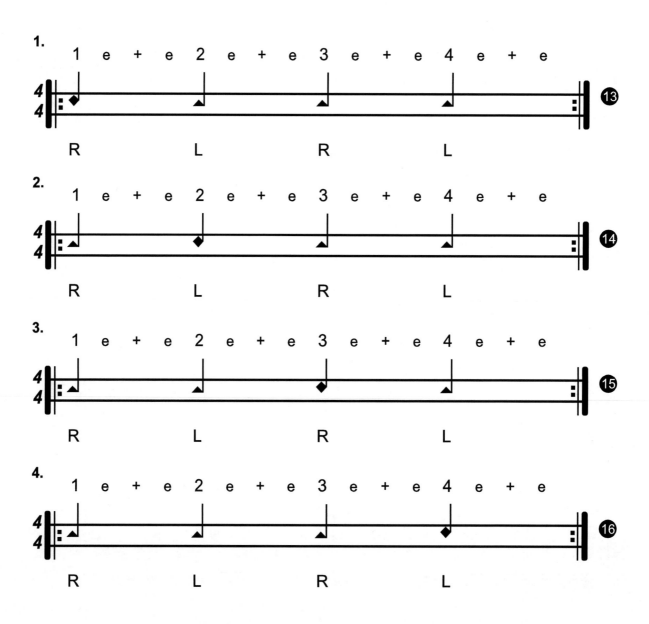

Accentuation, staggered accentuation

To accentuate a beat means to emphasize it by playing it louder.
Accents are denoted by this sign: ⟩

You can accentuate any beat that you wish. Here the accent moves through the bar in the course of the exercise - this is called staggered accentuation.

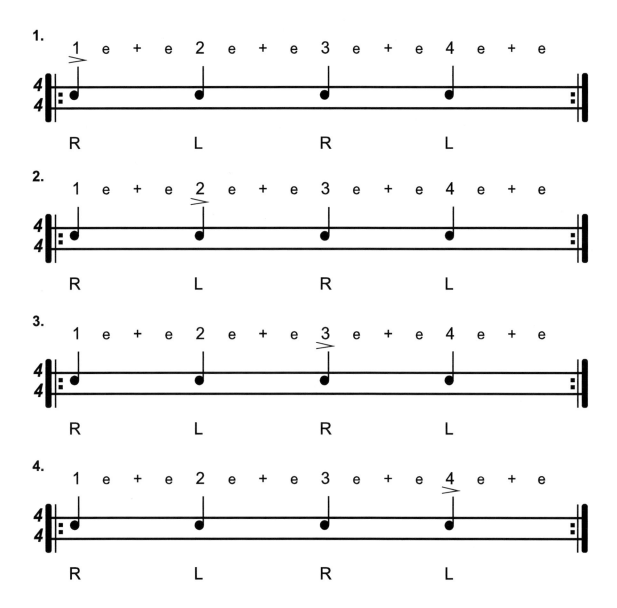

Staggered accentuation can be applied to the bass, the slap or the tap in exactly the same way.

Basic rhythmic exercises
in 4/4

The following exercises are designed with two goals in mind. First of all, they are intended to help you improve your sightreading abilities (playing from the sheet music).
Secondly, they will help you learn to coordinate the different beats. Start off playing them slowly before moving on to a moderate and finally to a fast tempo.

1.

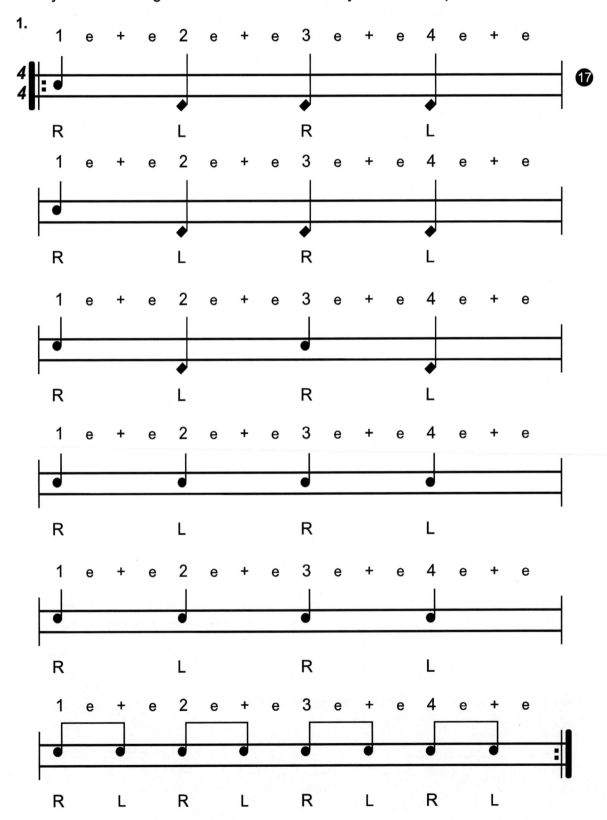

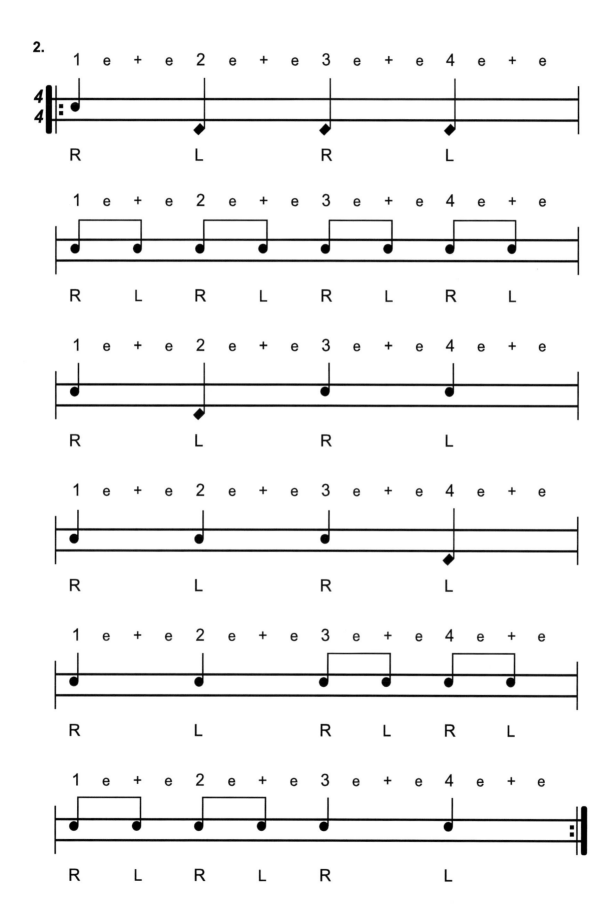

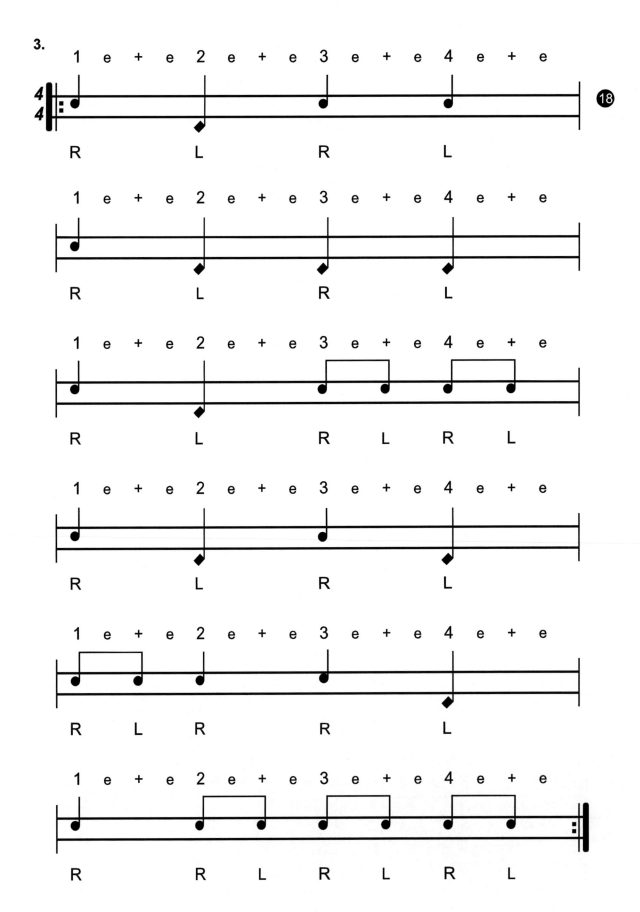

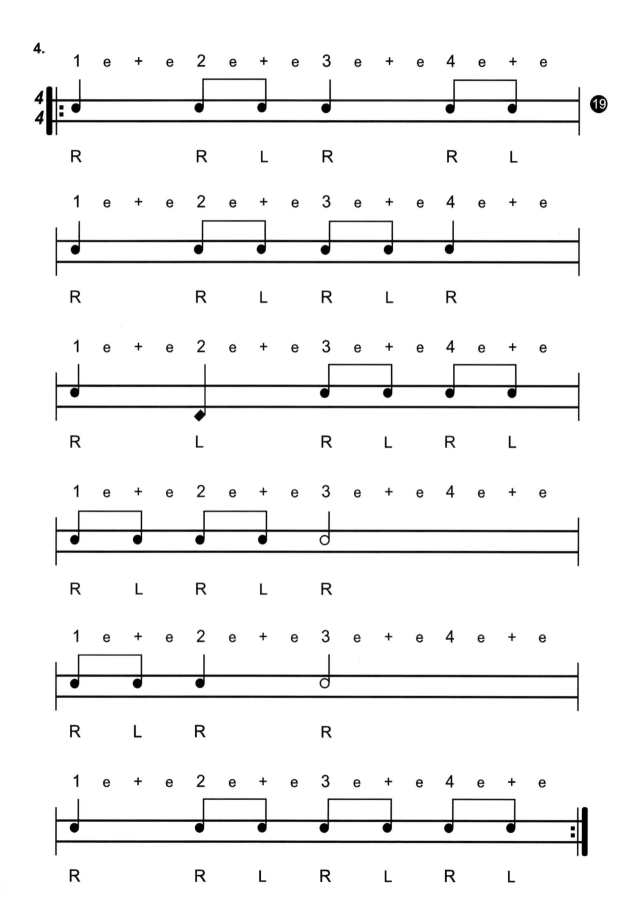

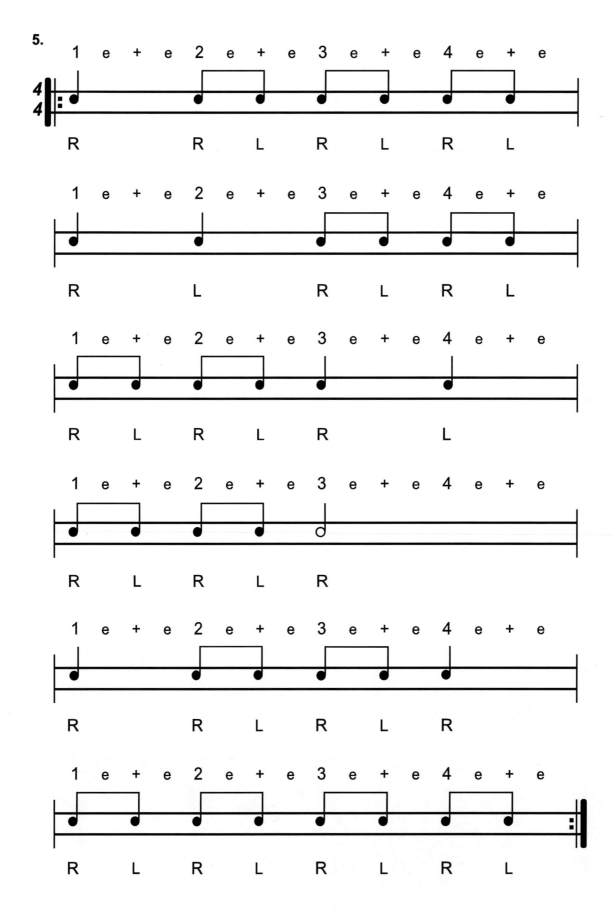

The following exercises contain rests (pauses). When practising, concentrate on keeping an exact rhythm and stick to a moderate tempo.

6.

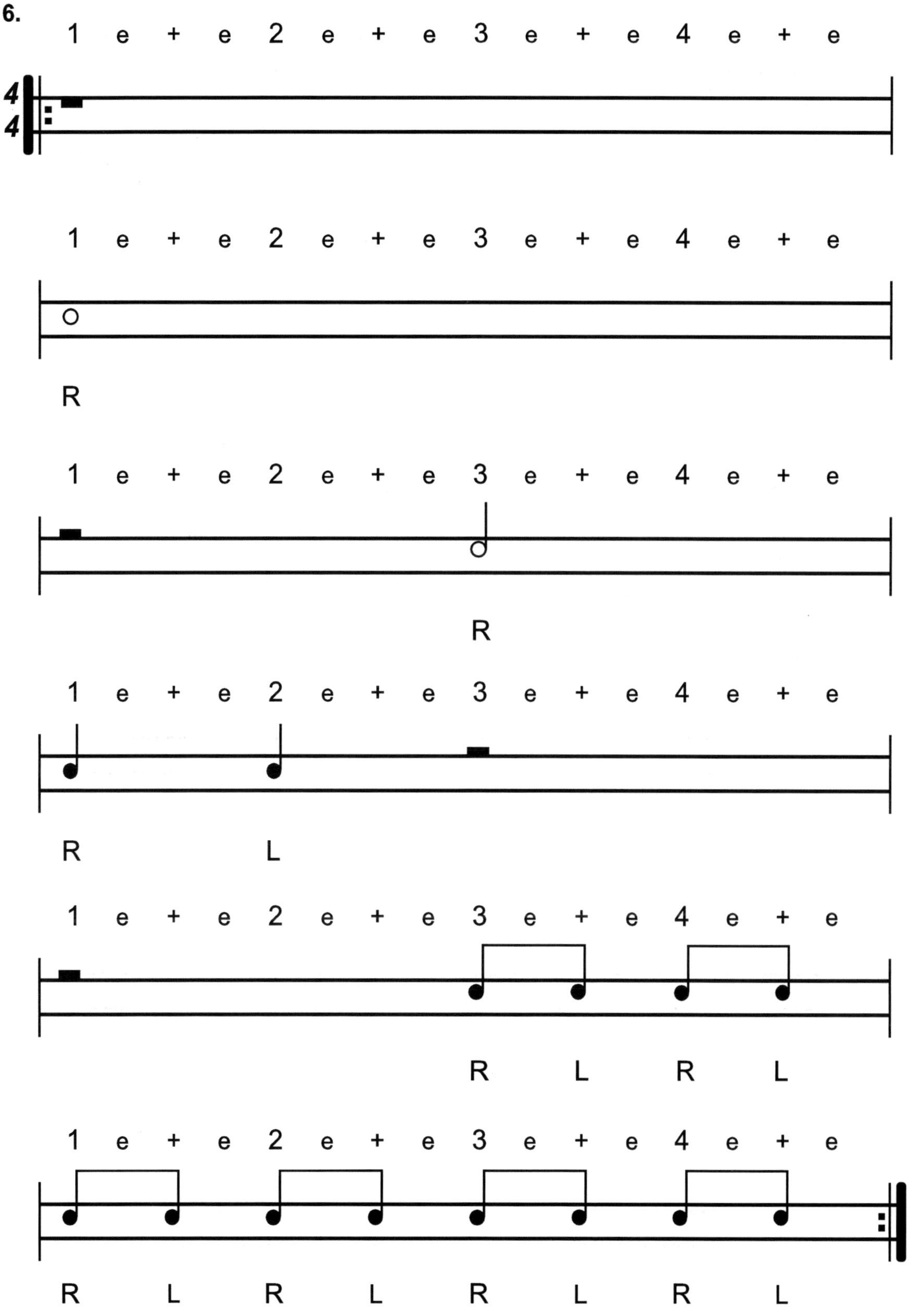

1　e　+　e　2　e　+　e　3　e　+　e　4　e　+　e

1　e　+　e　2　e　+　e　3　e　+　e　4　e　+　e

R

1　e　+　e　2　e　+　e　3　e　+　e　4　e　+　e

R

1　e　+　e　2　e　+　e　3　e　+　e　4　e　+　e

R　　　　　L

1　e　+　e　2　e　+　e　3　e　+　e　4　e　+　e

R　　L　　R　　L

1　e　+　e　2　e　+　e　3　e　+　e　4　e　+　e

R　　L　　R　　L　　R　　L　　R　　L

7.

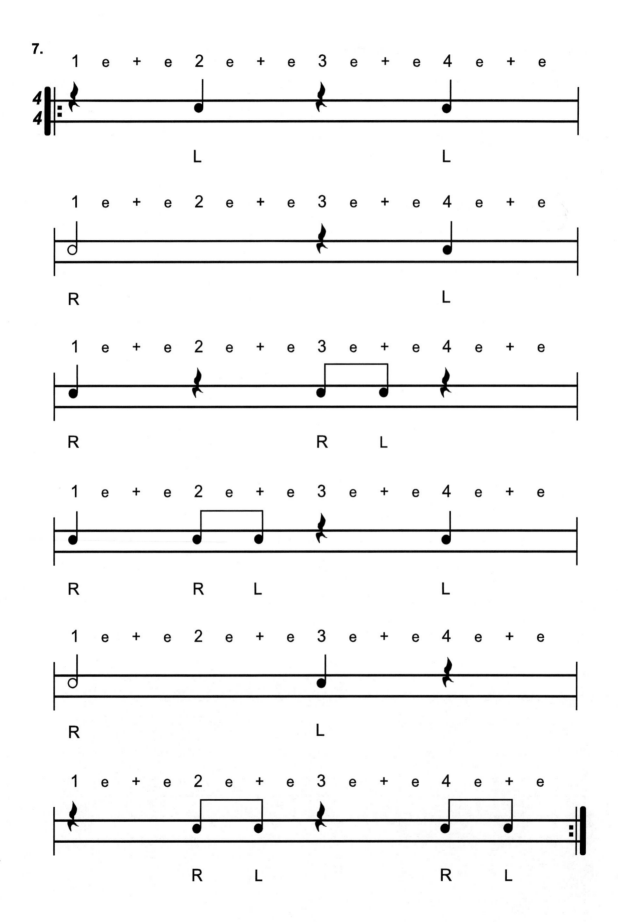

8.

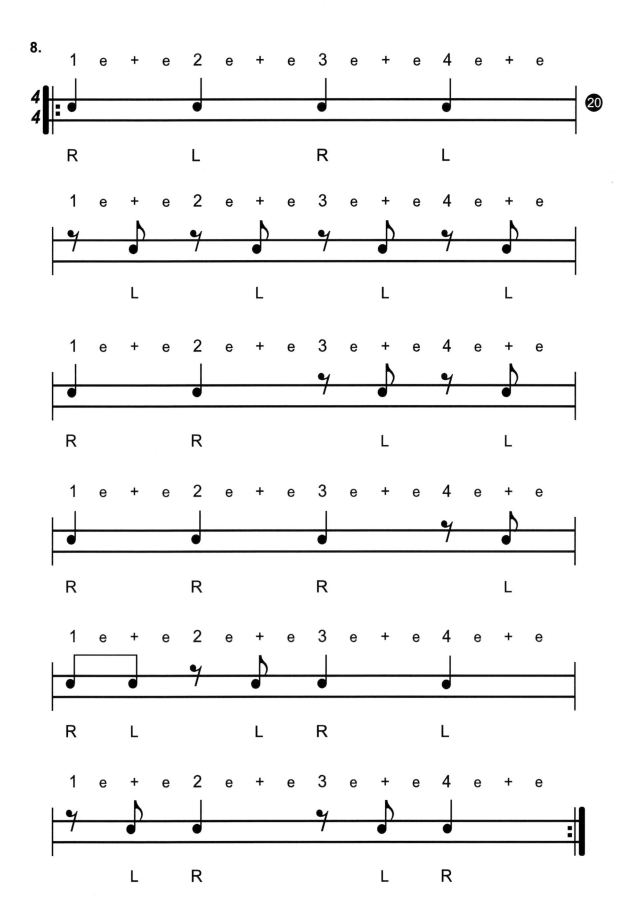

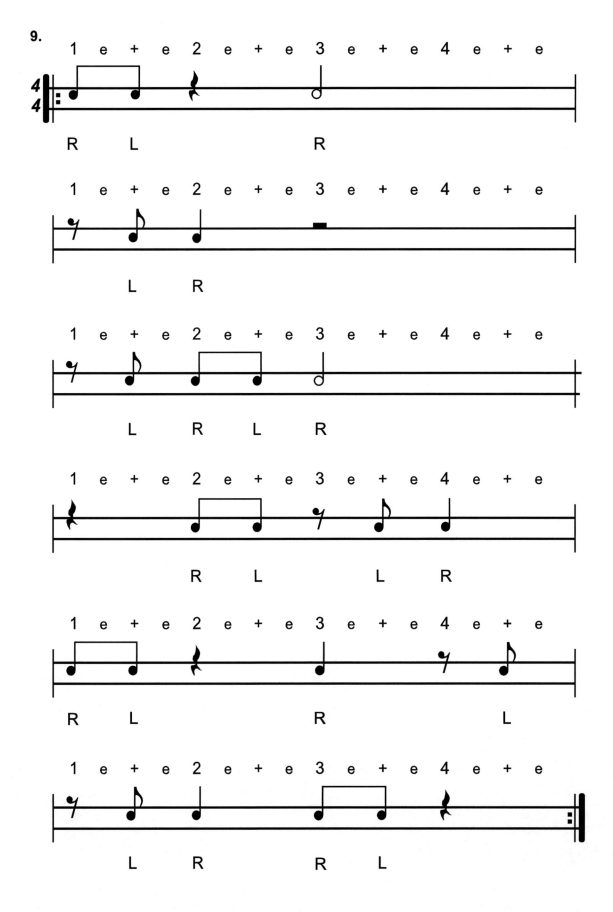

The following exercises contain 16th notes. Go through them one bar at a time before trying the complete exercise. Start with a slow tempo and only choose a faster one when you're sure of how they go.

10.

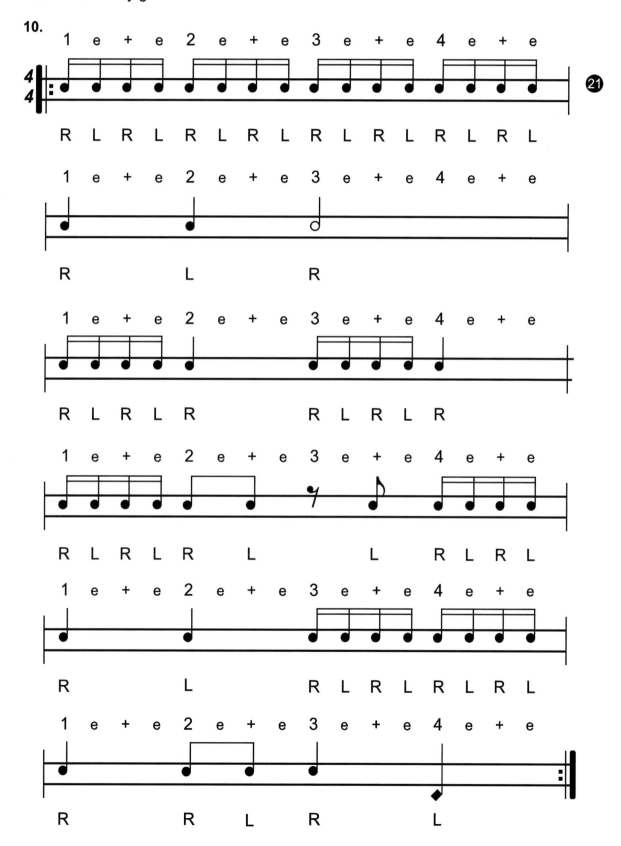

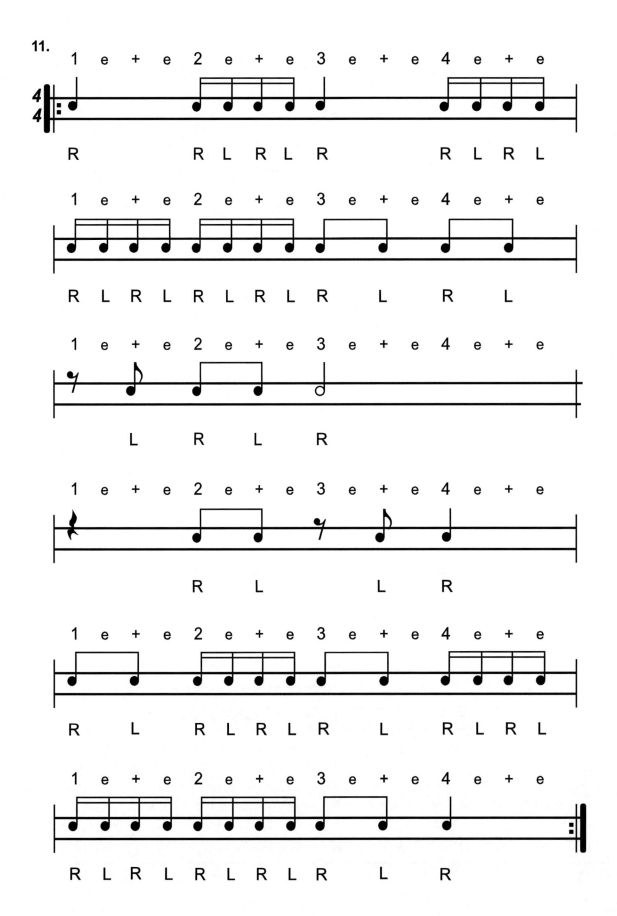

Basic rhythmic exercises
in 3/4

Now we're going to take a look at 3/4 time. The majority of rock, pop, jazz and Latin tunes are in 4/4, but of course exceptions prove the rule. Ternary rhythms such as 3/4 or 6/8 are used in numerous popular songs (e.g. "The House of the Rising Sun" or "Scarborough Fair") and of course in ballroom dancing and classical music (waltzes). Changing the meter in the course of a concert is a good way of adding variety to your music, so it's well worth while getting to know 3/4 time.

1.

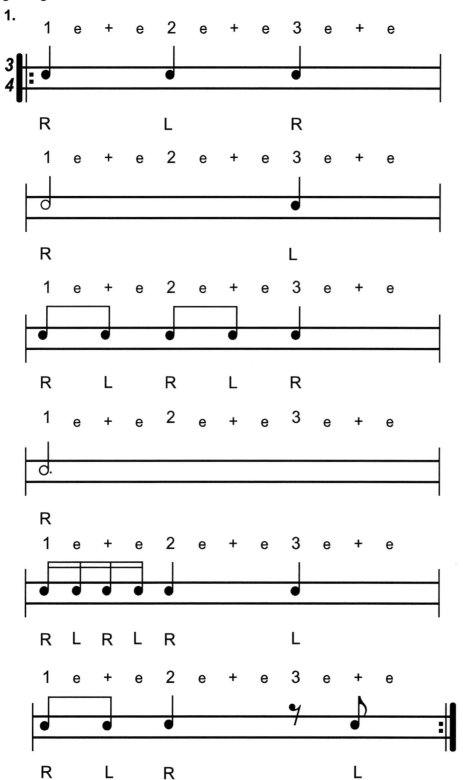

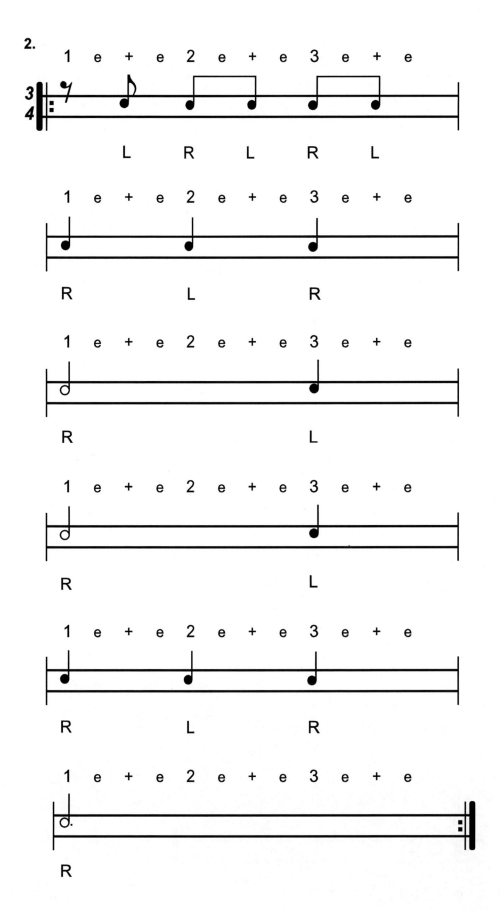

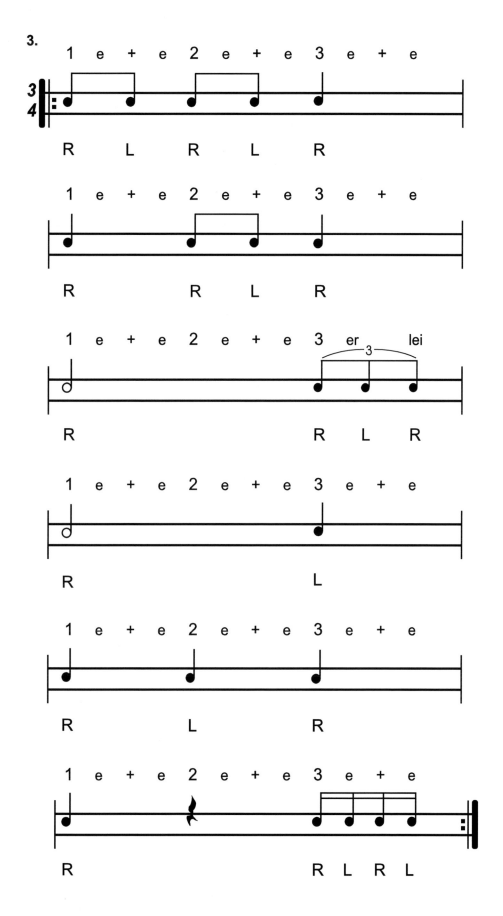

**Basic rhythmic exercises
in 2/4**

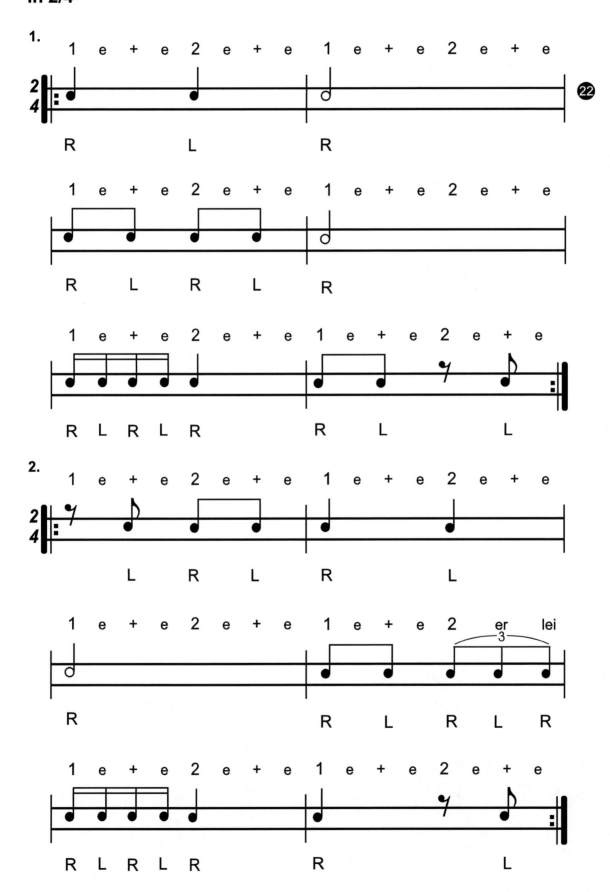

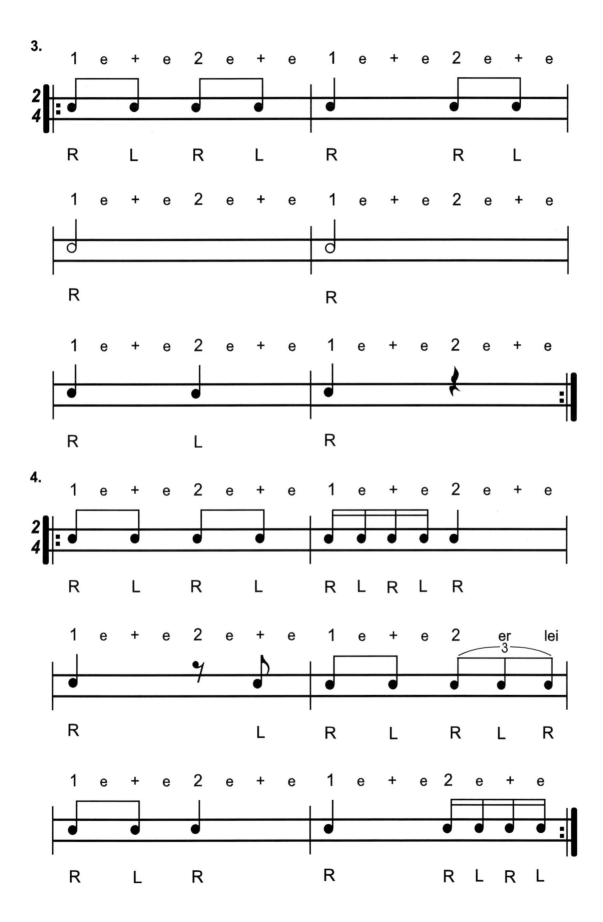

Basic triplet exercises

Triplets form the rhythmic basis for much roots music such as blues and reggae

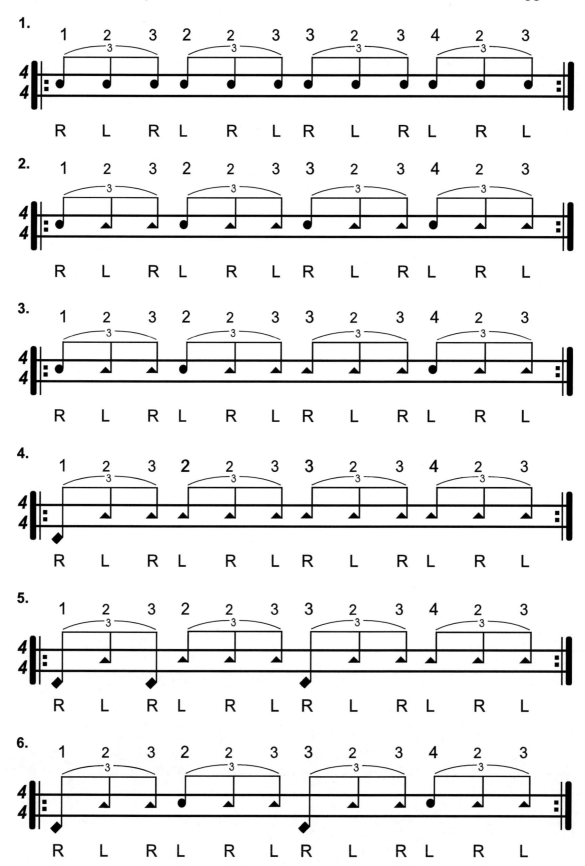

Groove Variations

One bar pop/rock grooves in 4/4

Play the one bar exercise and then repeat it twice, so that you play each rhythm three times altogether. Then leave a one bar pause before continuing with the groove. Most songs are made up of units such as the verse, bridge, middle eight or solo, which generally consist of 4- or 8-bar sequences.

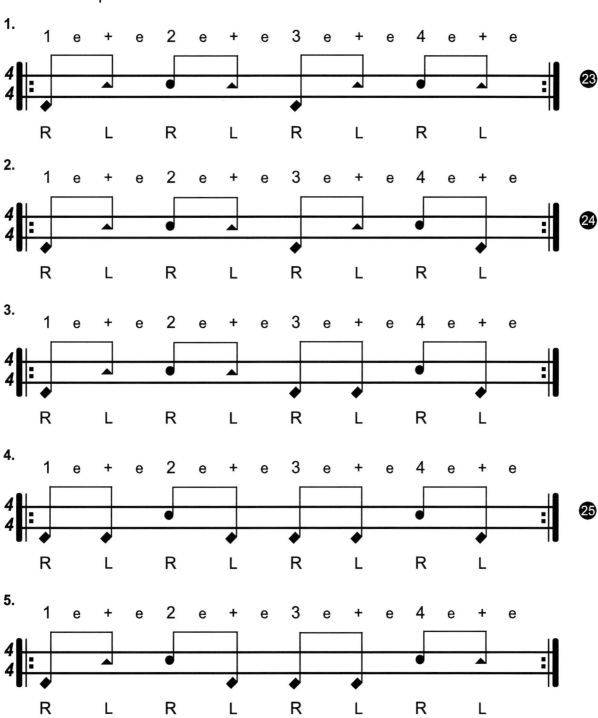

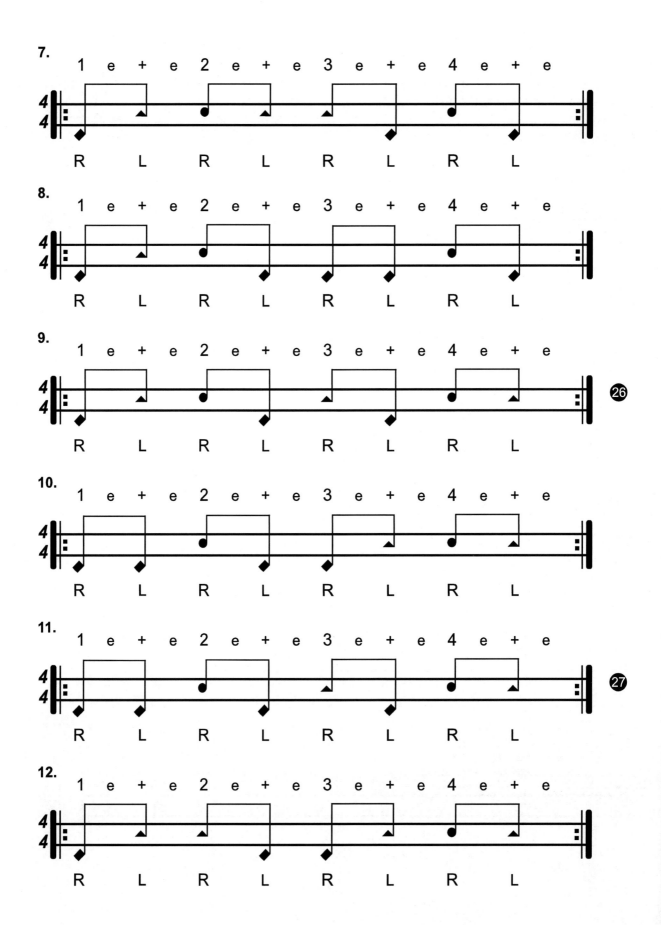

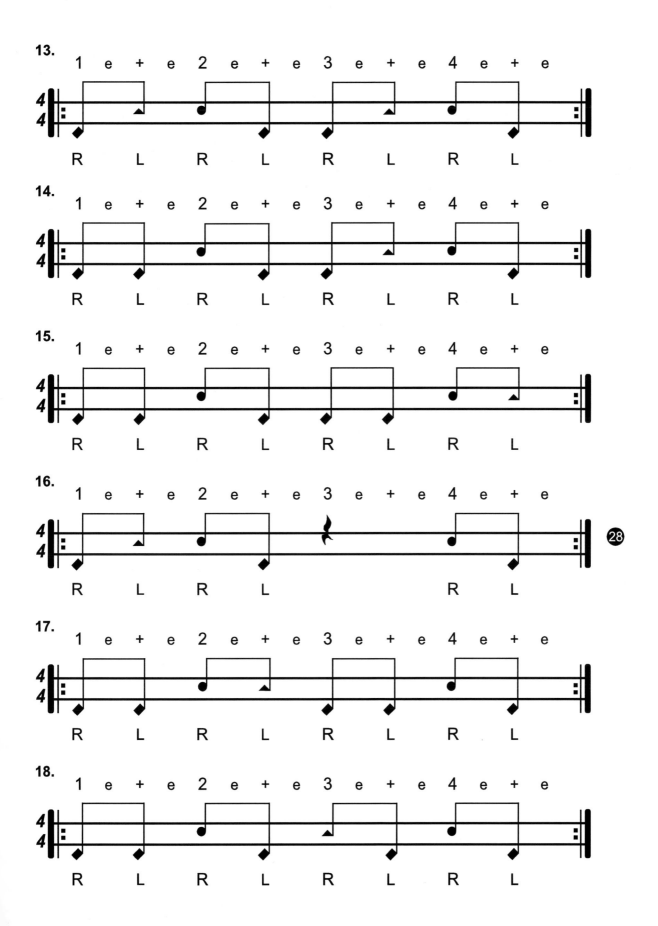

Two bar grooves in 4/4

Because they form a larger rhythmic unit, two bar grooves are more complex than one bar grooves. They have always been common in latin music, but nowadays are increasingly heard in rock and pop. By changing the order of the bars (playing bar two first and vice versa) you can create further rhythmic combinations.

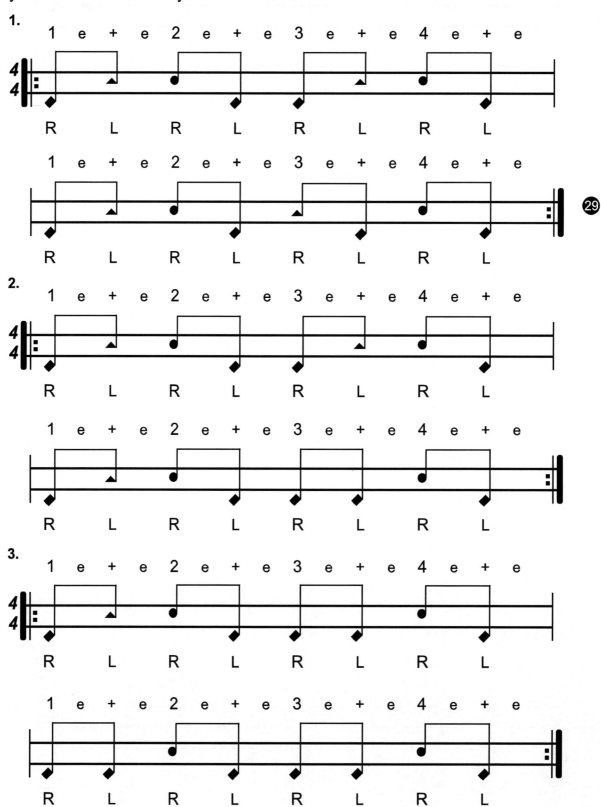

51

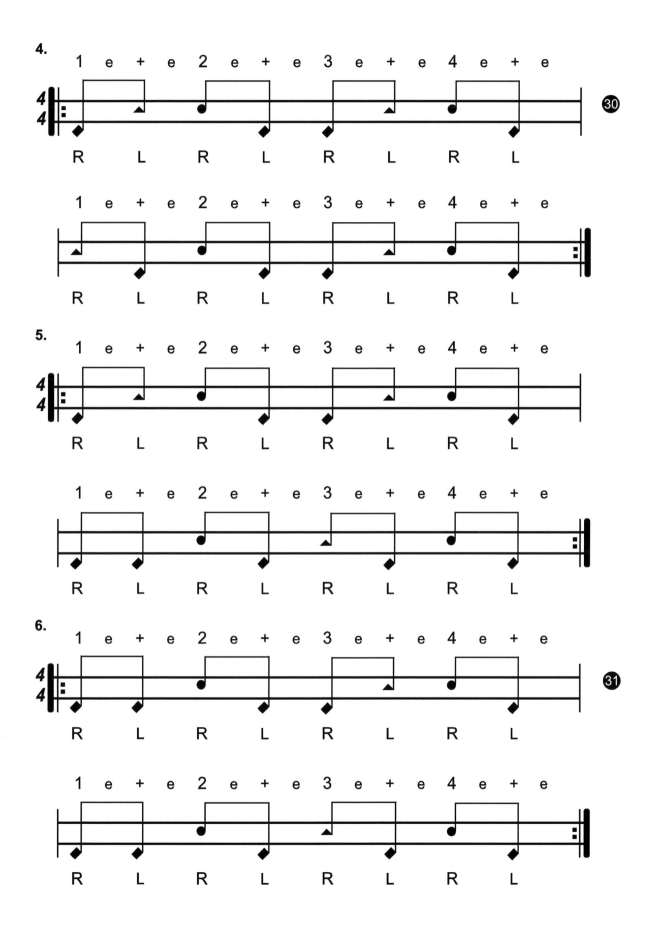

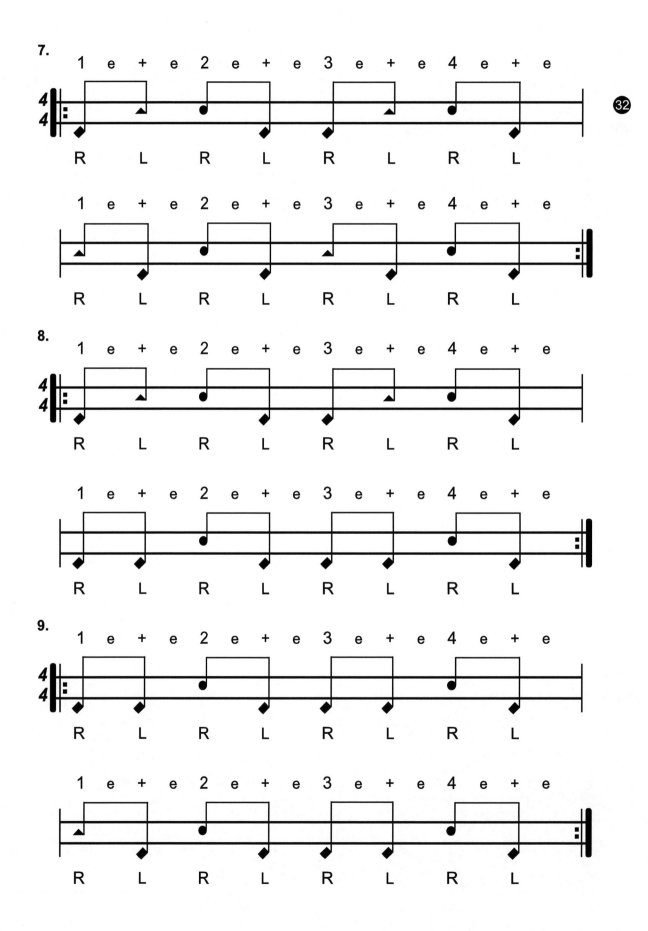

One bar grooves with eighth beat variations

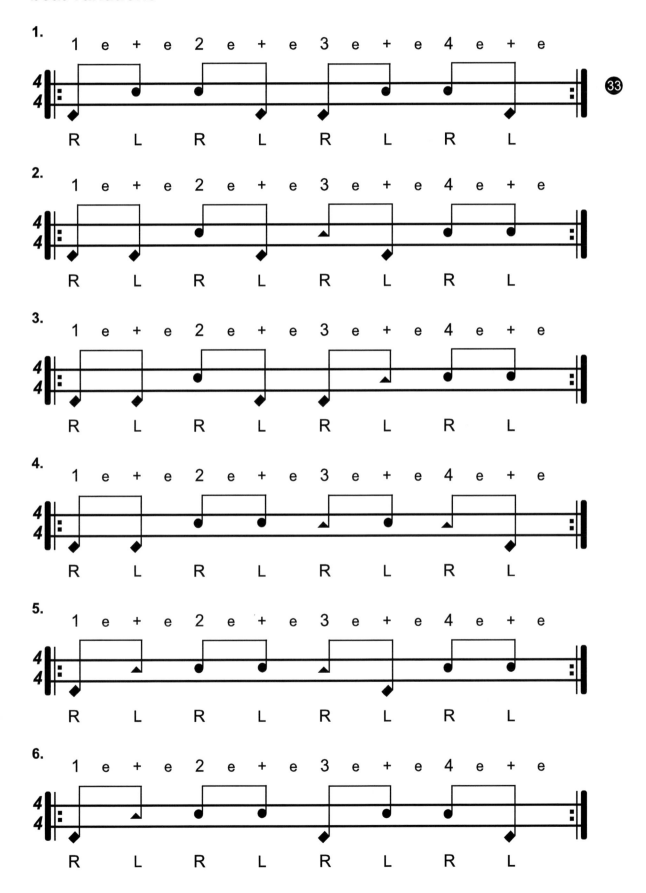

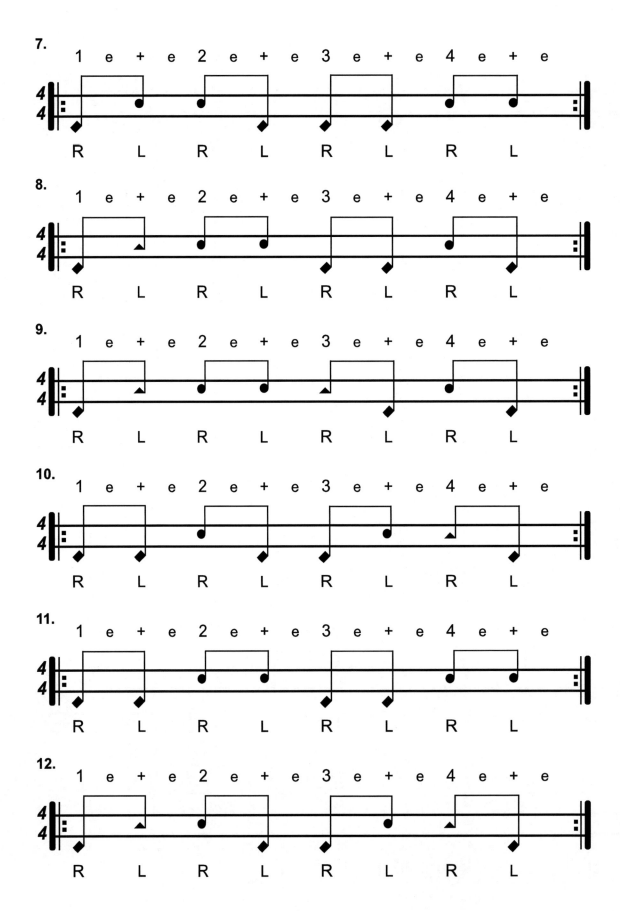

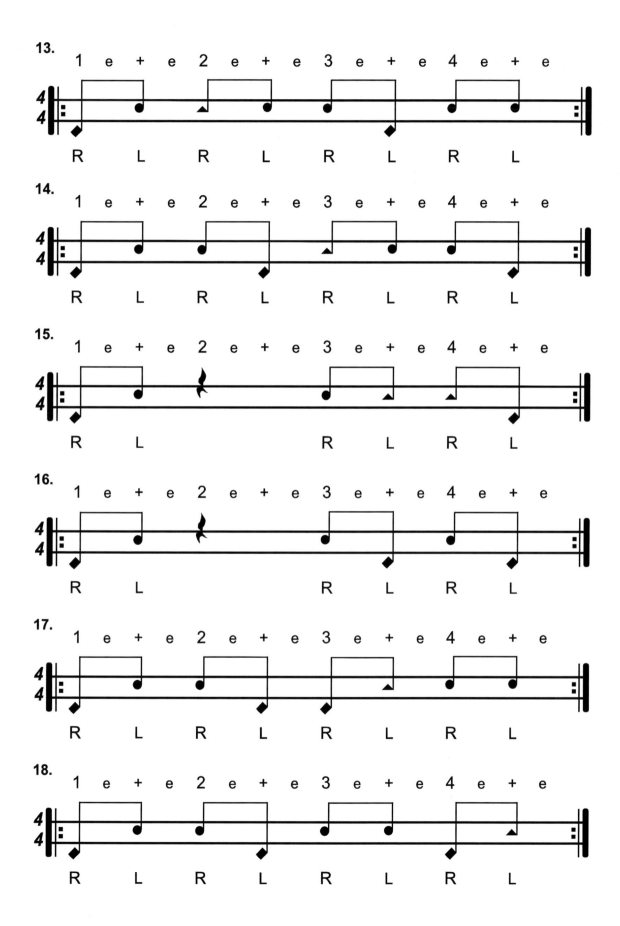

Two bar grooves in 3/4

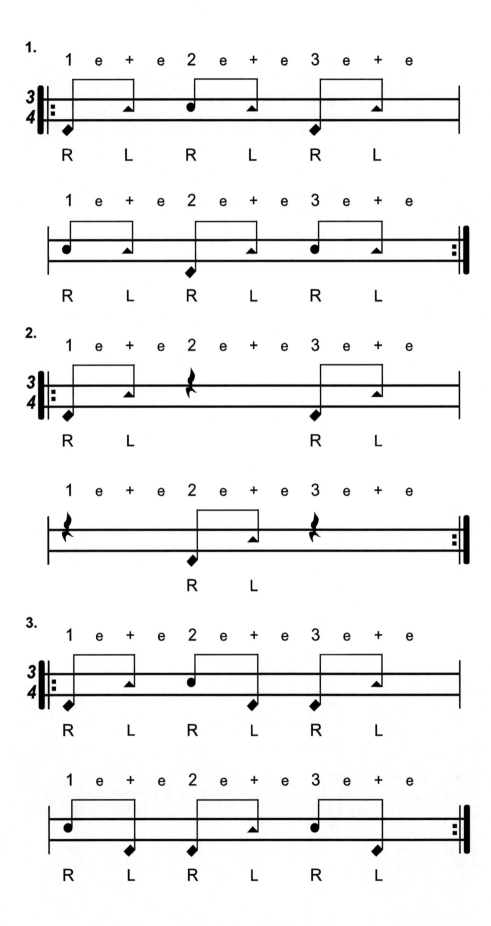

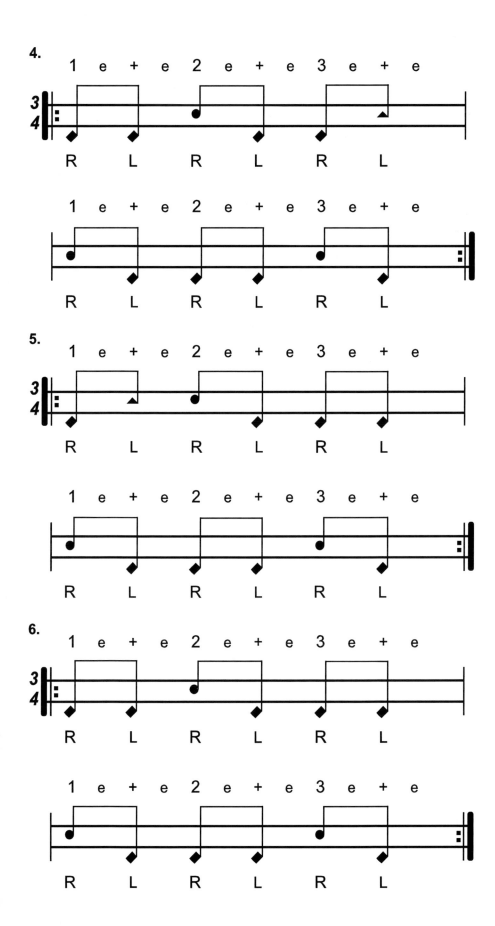

Grooves with Breaks

It's common practice to loosen up continuous grooves from time to time by means of so-called breaks. These do not occur at random and are generally placed so that they announce a transition from one part of a song to the next: 1) from intro into the verse, 2) before the next verse, 3) before the bridge, 4) before the solo and so on.
The cajon player's job is to deliver a grooving rhythm which also underlines the structure of the song.

Breaks

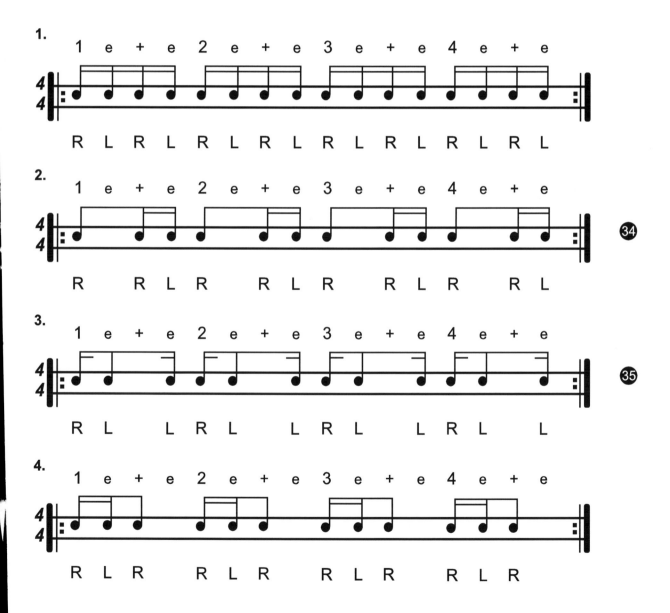

Break combinations

The breaks noted above can be played in any desired order to create new breaks.

For example:

1.

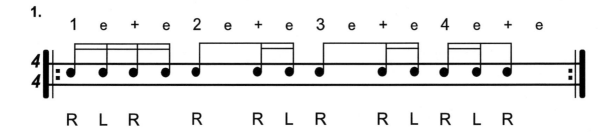

Grooves & breaks

Most songs and pieces of contemporary music can be broken down into intro, verse, refrain and bridge. Usually each unit can be further broken down into 4-bar sections - for example a 32-bar verse which is followed by a 16-bar refrain. As mentioned before, breaks are often used to announce the transition from one unit to the next. As a rhythm instrument player you don't necessarily orient yourself to the harmonic structure of a song, so it can be a great help to practise 4-bar sequences like these. Three bars groove and one bar break. Play these sequences as repeating cycles or loops. After a while you learn to feel intuitively when the 3 bars are over and it's time for the next break. The advantage of practising like this is that you learn to automatically play the breaks in the right places.

1.

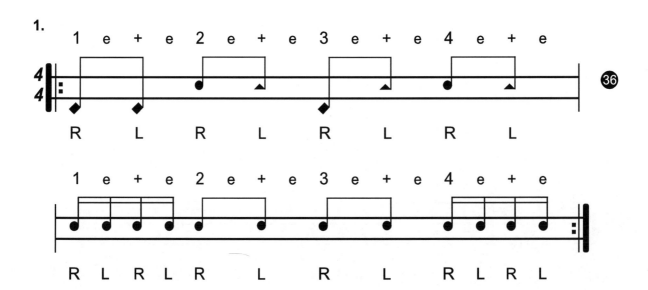

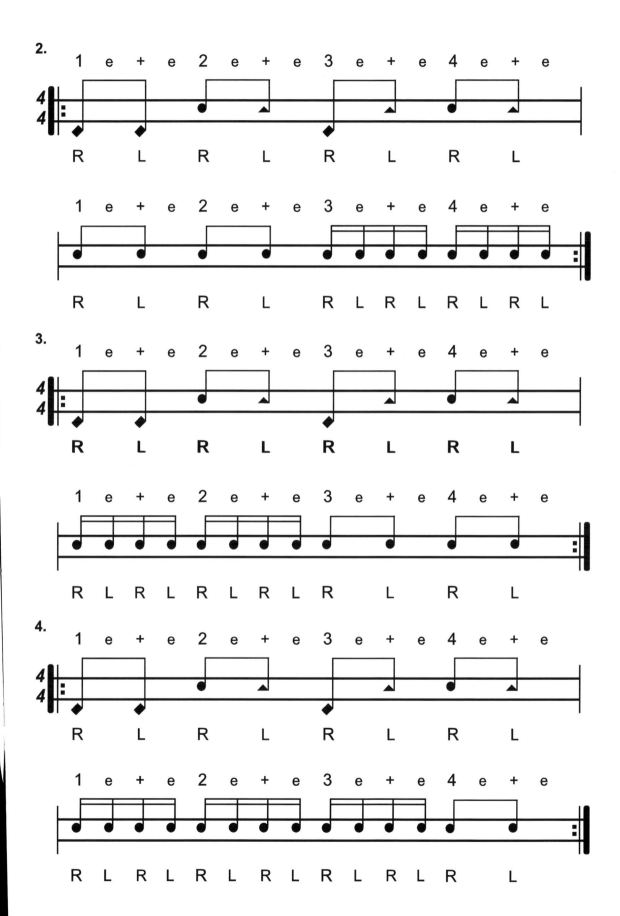

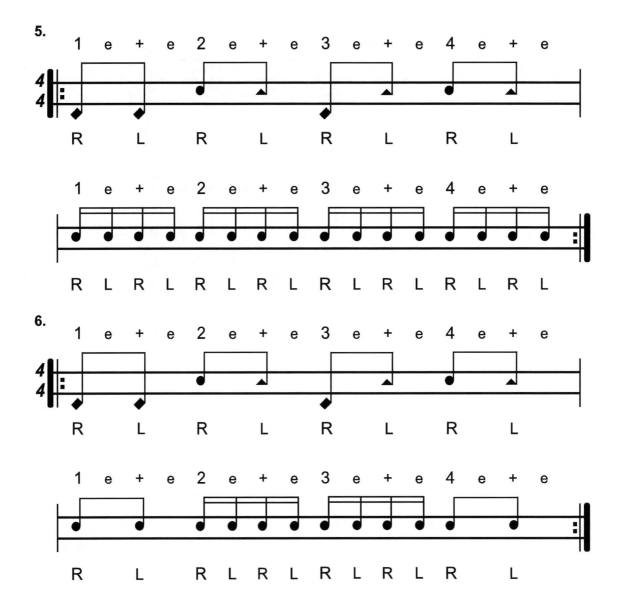

Play Along!

Introductory remarks

The 2nd part of this instruction book deals with playing in a band. Of course it's important to repeat and internalize all the basic exercises we've covered already. But above and beyond that, it's very important to learn how to play in an ensemble situation and accompany other musicians. The following titles are designed to get you playing along straight away.
Each song is found in two versions - the complete piece with cajon and a playback ("music minus you") for you to practise with.
Listen to the full version first and try to feel the groove, before you start playing along with the playback.

What are the main points to pay attention to when playing along? Well, the beginning of a piece is very important indeed. Where does the song actually start? This means that first of all you need to pay attention to the count-in or follow the lead-in (see the instructions for the inidvidual pieces). Concentrate on the meter and make sure you keep time with it (simple beat / level 1). When you feel comfortable doing this, you can move on to the variations shown (intermediate beat / level 2, more complex beat / level 3). At first you should try to play each of these three variations through the entire piece. When you succeed in mastering them individually, you can start combining them with one another. The transition from one to the next follows after 8, 12, 16 or 24 bars, depending on the verse form. The complete versions of the tunes clearly demonstrate how this works. It may take quite a while before you succeed in maintaining the basic groove (level 1) throughout the entire piece without mistakes. You shouldn't try to move on to the next level until you have mastered the previous one. Later, when you can play all three levels, it's important to learn to combine them. You can already listen to these combinations on the full versions of the tunes.

CD Track List

Recorded exercises

The exercises which can be heard on the CD are marked in the the notation with the

track numbers Tracks contain the playalongs.

Playalongs

Track ③⑦	Tennessee Blues	(with Cajon)
Track ③⑧	Tennessee Blues	(without Cajon)
Track ③⑨	Bossa Guitarra	(with Cajon)
Track ④⓪	Bossa Guitarra	(without Cajon)
Track ④①	Parlez-vous "Cajon"?	(with Cajon)
Track ④②	Parlez-vous "Cajon"?	(without Cajon)

Tennessee Blues

37 With Cajon

38 Without Cajon

Tennessee Blues (trad. / arr. Schell / Röttger)
This is a medium-tempo country number.
It begins with a lead-in from the guitar (- 2,3,4,)
and you start on the following "1".
The tune continues without any breaks through four 16-bar verses (no bridge).

Simple beat (level 1)

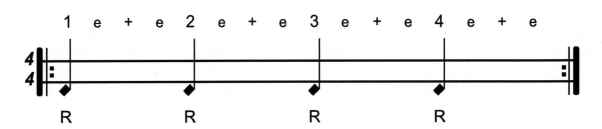

Intermediate beat (level 2)

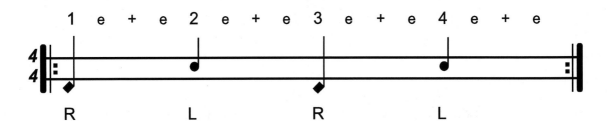

More complex beat (level 3)

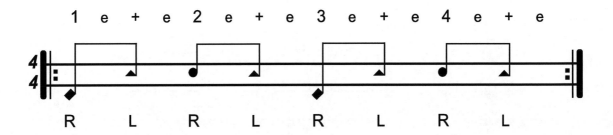

Bossa Guitarra

39 With Cajon

40 Without Cajon

Bossa Guitarra (Felix Schell)
This piece is a real Bossa Nova with that typical South American flair.
We begin with a slap on the "4" - 1, 2, 3, "slap" and the piece itself starts
with the rhythm guitar on the following "1". Bossa Guitarra employs an AABA form.
Note: at the end of the B part (bridge) there is a break, you need to be ready for it.

Simple beat (level 1)

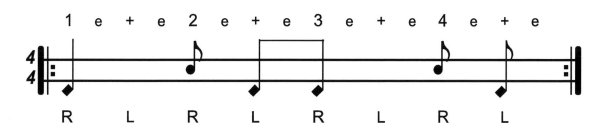

Intermediate beat (level 2)

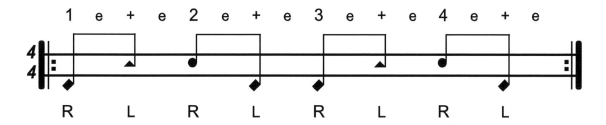

More complex beat (level 3)

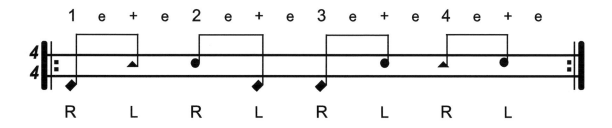

Parlez-vous "Cajon"?

41 With Cajon

42 Without Cajon

Parlez-vous "Cajon"? (Schell / Röttger)
This tune has a funky feel. The verse form has 12 bars
and is simply repeated a number of times.
There are no breaks and no bridge.

Simple beat (level 1)

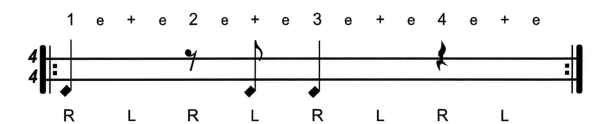

Intermediate beat (level 2)

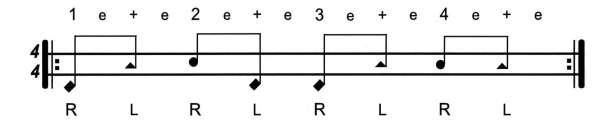

More complex beat (level 3)

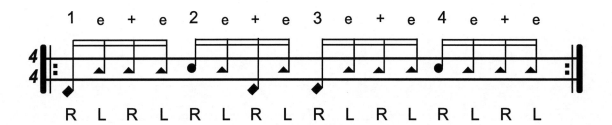